Sequoyah
and the Written Word

Kelly Rodgers

Consultants

Regina Holland, Ed.S., *Henry County Schools;*
Christina Noblet, Ed.S., *Paulding County School District;* **Jennifer Troyer,** *Paulding County Schools;* **David Proctor,** *Muscogee (Creek) Cultural Advisor;* **John Ross,** *Certified Cherokee Language Teacher;* **Karen Coody Cooper, M.A.**, *Cherokee Historian*

Publishing Credits

Rachelle Cracchiolo, M.S.Ed., *Publisher*
Conni Medina, M.A.Ed., *Managing Editor*
Emily R. Smith, M.A.Ed., *Series Developer*
Diana Kenney, M.A.Ed., NBCT, *Content Director*
Torrey Maloof, *Editor*
Courtney Patterson, *Multimedia Designer*

Image Credits: Cover background Gerry Embleton / North Wind Picture Archives; pp. 7, 22–24, 26, 32 Alamy; pp. 3, 5 Courtesy of Archives of the Southern Highland Craft Guild and Western Carolina University Hunter Library Digital Collections; pp. front cover, 1, 6, 16 Courtesy of Penelope Johnson Allen Cherokee Collection 1775–1878, Tennessee State Library and Archives; p. 21 Courtesy of the Cherokee Phoenix newspaper; p. 9 Getty Images; pp. 3, 21 LOC [LC-USZ62-115660]; p.13 LOC [LC-USZ62-3483]; pp.20, 29 LOC [LC-USZ62-61141]; p. 8 Science Source; p. 12 The Granger Collection; p. 12, 15, 18, 29 Yoshiko Miyake/Cricket Media/Carus Publishing Company; All other images from iStock and/ or Shutterstock.

Library of Congress Cataloging-in-Publication Data

Names: Rodgers, Kelly.
Title: Sequoyah and the written word / Kelly Rodgers.
Description: Huntington Beach, CA : Teacher Created Materials, [2016] |
  Includes index. | Audience: Grades K-3.?
Identifiers: LCCN 2015042466 | ISBN 9781493825547 (pbk.)
Subjects: LCSH: Sequoyah, 1770?-1843--Juvenile literature. | Cherokee
  Indians--Biography--Juvenile literature. | Cherokee language--Writing--Juvenile literature. | Cherokee language--Alphabet--Juvenile literature.
Classification: LCC E99.C5 R59 2016 | DDC 973.04975570092--dc23
LC record available at http://lccn.loc.gov/2015042466

Teacher Created Materials

5301 Oceanus Drive
Huntington Beach, CA 92649-1030
http://www.tcmpub.com

ISBN 978-1-4938-2554-7

© 2017 Teacher Created Materials, Inc.
Printed in China
Nordica.082019.CA21901024

Table of Contents

27

A Changing World

It was the early 1800s. Georgia was changing quickly. New **settlers** were pouring in. Some wanted land. Others were searching for gold. But there was another group of people there, too. They were not new. This group had been living there a long time. They were worried about their future. These people were the Cherokee (CHER-uh-kee).

The Cherokee had their own **culture**. They lived by their own rules. They spoke their own language. They had unique (yoo-NEEK) beliefs and **customs**. Their way of life was very different from how the new settlers lived. The Cherokee did not want this to change.

Miners search for gold along the Yahoola River.

Finger weaving is a cultural tradition that is still done today.

A Cherokee man had a plan. His name was Sequoyah (sih-KWOY-uh). He wanted to help his people. He wanted them to move into the modern world. But he also tried to help **preserve** their culture. He thought his people could do both. They just had to learn some new skills.

He wanted to teach his people to read and write. But he wanted them to do it in their own language. He would create the written language himself. Some thought this was a good idea. Others thought Sequoyah was being foolish.

Don't Forget!

Long ago, the Cherokee did not have a written language. They told stories over and over so that the stories would live on.

Sequoyah

Cherokee culture has stayed strong over the years and includes art, clothing, and music.

This is a re-created Cherokee summer house.

Young Sequoyah

We do not know much about the young Sequoyah. Many say he was born around 1770. He lived in a Cherokee village. It is said to have been in what is now Tennessee (ten-nuh-SEE). His mother was Cherokee. There are different ideas about his father.

Some say his father was white. He may have been in the army. Others say he was half white and half Cherokee. He may have been a fur trader. No one knows for sure. The records are not clear. But we do know that Sequoyah was raised as a Cherokee.

American Indian fur traders

Sequoyah had many skills. He was a hunter. He was a trader. He was also a **blacksmith**. Through his work, he met many new settlers. He saw how they **communicated**. They used written words. He saw the importance of reading and writing.

Sequoyah thought about making a writing system. It would be for the Cherokee language. He thought it would help his people. They could write their laws. They could keep records. They could spread news more easily. Some of his friends thought the idea was crazy. They made fun of him. He started to work on the system in 1809.

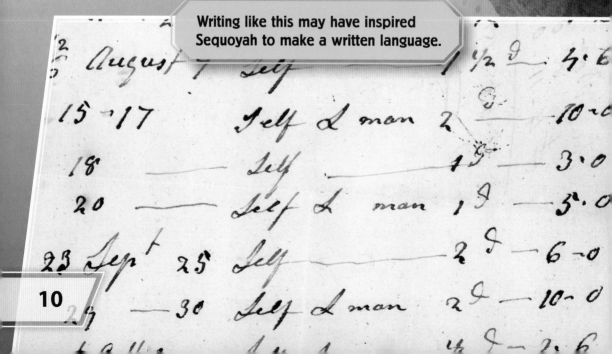

Writing like this may have inspired Sequoyah to make a written language.

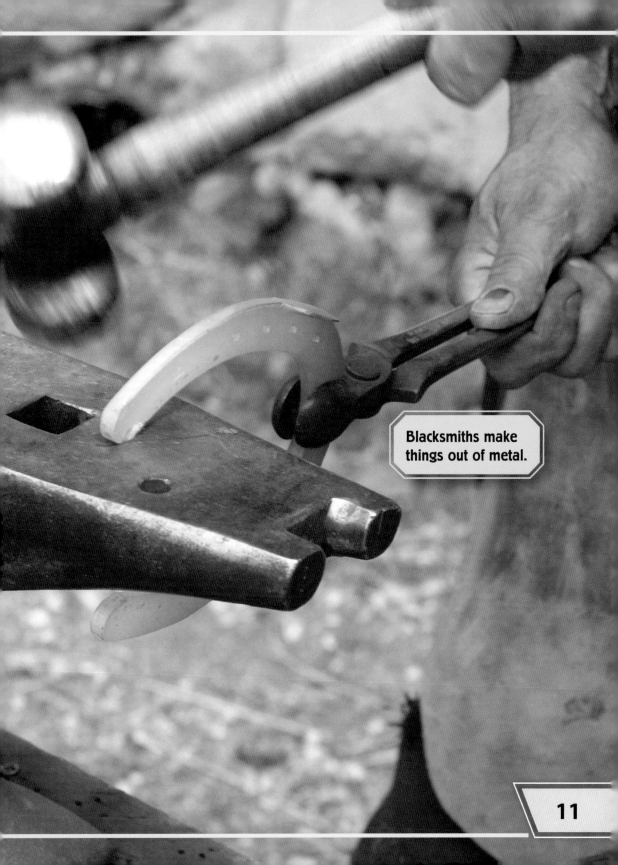

Blacksmiths make things out of metal.

A Letter Home

In 1812, a war broke out. Sequoyah became a soldier. He fought for the United States. During the war, he saw other men writing letters home. He wished he could write letters, too. But he did not know English.

He also saw that the white men could read **military** orders. He could not do this. Nor could the other Cherokee men. He knew his world was changing. He wanted to help his people. He kept working on his new system.

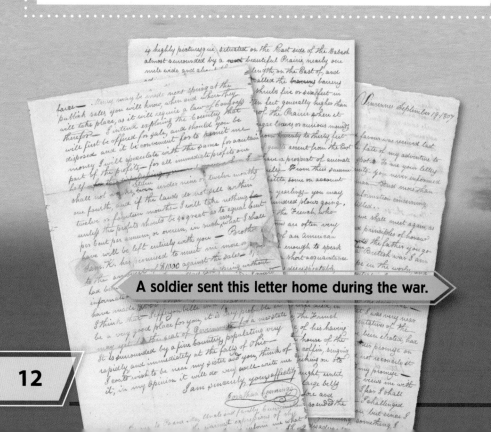

A soldier sent this letter home during the war.

War of 1812

The War of 1812 was fought between the United States and Great Britain. It was about shipping and trade on the seas.

Teach Me!

After the war, Sequoyah returned home. He continued to work on the system. He drew symbols. Each one stood for a sound. These symbols made sense to Sequoyah. But would they make sense to others?

Sequoyah needed someone else to learn the meanings of the symbols. This was the only way he could be sure that his writing system worked. He wondered who would be willing to learn his new language. Then one day, his daughter came to him. Her name was Ayoka (i-OH-kuh). She asked him to explain the strange drawings he had made.

Family Man

Sequoyah married a Cherokee woman in 1815. Her name was Sally Benge. Sally was Ayoka's mother.

Sequoyah made up a game. He used the game to teach the symbols to Ayoka. He explained each symbol. She understood most of them. But she had some questions, too. Some of the symbols were confusing.

The father and daughter began to work together as a team. They worked hard. They improved the written language. But there was a problem.

Some people thought Sequoyah's writing was witchcraft. Others said it did not work. Sequoyah had to prove that the symbols could be read. He thought of a clever way to do this!

This letter was written by Sequoyah's cousin with the Cherokee symbols and was sent to Cherokee Chief John Ross in 1838.

D _o_	R _e_	T _i_	Ꮷ _o_	O _u_	i _v_
S _ga_ Ꭴ _ka_	Ᏺ _ge_	Y _gi_	A _go_	J _gu_	E _gv_
Ꮙ _ha_	P _he_	Ꭾ _hi_	Ꮶ _ho_	Ꮡ _hu_	Ꮽ _hv_
W _la_	Ꮁ _le_	Ꮄ _li_	G _lo_	M _lu_	Ꮧ _lv_
Ꮉ _ma_	Ꮀ _me_	H _mi_	Ꮽ _mo_	Ꭹ _mu_	
Ꮎ _na_ Ꮳ _hna_ G _nah_	Ʌ _ne_	Ꮒ _ni_	Z _no_	Ꮖ _nu_	Ꮓ _nv_
Ꮖ _qua_	Ꮃ _que_	Ꮅ _qui_	V _quo_	Ꮘ _quu_	Ꮛ _quv_
Ꮜ _sa_ Ꮝ _s_	Ꮞ _se_	Ꮈ _si_	Ꮰ _so_	Ꮢ _su_	R _sv_
Ꮣ _da_ W _ta_	Ꮥ _de_ Ꮦ _te_	Ꮧ _di_ Ꮨ _ti_	V _do_	Ꮪ _du_	Ꮫ _dv_
Ꮬ _dla_ Ꮭ _tla_	Ꮮ _tle_	C _tli_	Ꮼ _tlo_	Ꮯ _tlu_	P _tlv_
Ꮳ _tsa_	Ꮴ _tse_	Ꮵ _tsi_	K _tso_	Ꮶ _tsu_	Ꮴ _tsv_
G _wa_	Ꮺ _we_	Ꮻ _wi_	Ꮼ _wo_	Ꮹ _wu_	6 _wv_
Ꮿ _ya_	B _ye_	Ꭿ _yi_	Ꭹ _yo_	G _yu_	B _yv_

Sequoyah went to a meeting. He took Ayoka with him. But she stayed outside. He asked the meeting's leaders to tell him a few words. He wrote them down using his symbols. Then, the note was taken outside to Ayoka. She was able to read what they had said inside. The plan had worked!

Sequoyah used this meeting to improve the system even more. He stopped making symbols for words. He made them for sounds instead. After 12 years of working on the system, there were 86 symbols. He had done it! He had created a written language.

Fed Up!

It wasn't easy for Sequoyah to create the symbols. Once, his wife wanted him to stop working. She threw his papers in the fire! He lost two years worth of work. He had to start over.

ᏞᎻᏃᏠᏆᎣᎦᏣ ᏎᎵᏰᏉᎦᎶᏨᏔᎻᏨ

Sequoyah taught the written language to others. He felt this was a big step for his people. Soon, many of them could read and write. They were now the first American Indians to have a written language.

Things began to change. The tribe wrote their laws. They made a **constitution** (KAHN-stuh-TOO-shuhn). They kept records. They **translated** books. They even had their own newspaper!

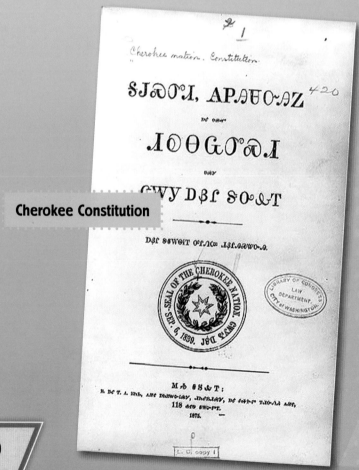

Cherokee Constitution

ᏣᎳᎩ ᏧᎶᏫᏍᎩ

CHEROKEE PHOENIX.

VOL. I. NEW ECHOTA, THURSDAY APRIL 10, 1828. NO. ?

(Historic newspaper body text, largely illegible, printed in columns with portions in Cherokee syllabary.)

Read All About It!

The Cherokee's newspaper is called the *Cherokee Phoenix* (FEE-niks). You can read the modern-day version on the Internet.

CHEROKEE PHOENIX

News   Culture   Opinion   Multimedia   Election   About Us

6 Tribal Councilors say goodbye

BY JAMI MURPHY
Reporter
08/19/2015 12:00 PM

TAHLEQUAH, Okla. – On Aug. 10, six outgoing Tribal Councilors, who either termed out or gave up their seat, were honored with plaques during their last day of meetings.

Former Tribal Council Speaker Tina Glory Jordan thanked her constituents for... **Read More**

Tribal Council Speaker Tina Glory Jordan receives a plaque and gavel from Deputy Chief S. Joe Crittenden on Aug. 10 at the Tribal Complex in Tahlequah, Oklahoma. Each of the six outgoing Tribal Councilors received plaques. JAMI MURPHY/CHEROKEE PHOENIX

Georgia Chapter of Trail of Tears Association to meet Sept. 12

BY STAFF REPORTS
08/19/2015 10:00 AM

DAHLONEGA, Ga. – The September meeting of the Georgia Chapter of the Trail of Tears Association will be held from 10:30 a.m. to noon on Sept. 12 at Kennesaw Mountain Battlefield Park in the Educational Center. **Read More**

Quick Search...

Culture
CN accepting history tours grant applications
BY STAFF REPORTS
08/13/2015 10:00 AM

TAHLEQUAH, Okla. – Through an education tour grant program, Cherokee Nation Cultural Tourism is awarding grants to increase the experience and... **Read More**

Education
CN concurrent enrollment scholarship deadline is Sept. 9
BY STAFF REPORTS
08/17/2015 12:00 PM

TAHLEQUAH, Okla. – High school students wanting to apply for the Cherokee Nation College Resource Center concurrent enrollment... **Read More**

Be Prepared! Accidents happen!

Enroll your Native Teen in CHIP (Child Health Insurance Program) and have coverage when you need it.

Call Indian Health Care Resource Center of Tulsa at 918-382-1219 and ask to speak to a Benefits Coordinator today!

The written language gave the Cherokee a new life. It was special. It belonged to them. Now, they could write their thoughts. They could share ideas. They could express their feelings on paper. They could record their past. History would not be forgotten.

school sign

Sequoyah felt his written language was special for other reasons, too. He thought it would show that his people were making progress. They were moving forward. He hoped this would earn them respect from the U.S. government (GUHV-uhrn-muhnt). Sadly, it did not.

street signs

Cherokee Writing Today

Today, Sequoyah's symbols can be seen in many places. They are on street signs and schools. They are used to write songs and letters. They are used to communicate in many ways.

Forced Out

In 1838, the U.S. government forced the Cherokee off their lands. The government made them move west to Oklahoma. At that time it was called Indian Territory. They did not want to go, but they had no choice.

The Cherokee did not get to pack their things. They were forced to walk thousands of miles. It took months. Troops treated them badly on the march. Many people got sick along the way. More than 5,000 died. The long walk came to be known as the Trail of Tears.

A Nation within a Nation

In 1794, the Cherokee Nation was formed. It is a nation within the United States! Its citizens are proud of their culture and history.

Honoring Sequoyah

Sequoyah lived a unique life. His world changed quickly. He tried to change with it. He also tried to help his people. He gave them a special gift. It was the gift of writing. That gift helped the Cherokee preserve their past.

Today, Sequoyah is thought of as a hero. His name is honored in many places. Mount Sequoyah in the Great Smoky Mountains is named after him. Several schools share his name. Sequoyah was a special man. He lives on in the hearts and minds of people everywhere.

In 1980, Sequoyah was honored with a postage stamp.

the Great Smoky Mountains

This is a trail on Mount Sequoyah.

Try It!

Sequoyah created symbols for sounds. Make up your own symbols. Draw symbols to represent sounds or words. Make a chart that shows which symbol stands for each word or sound. Write a letter to a friend with your symbols. Have your friend use the chart to read your letter!

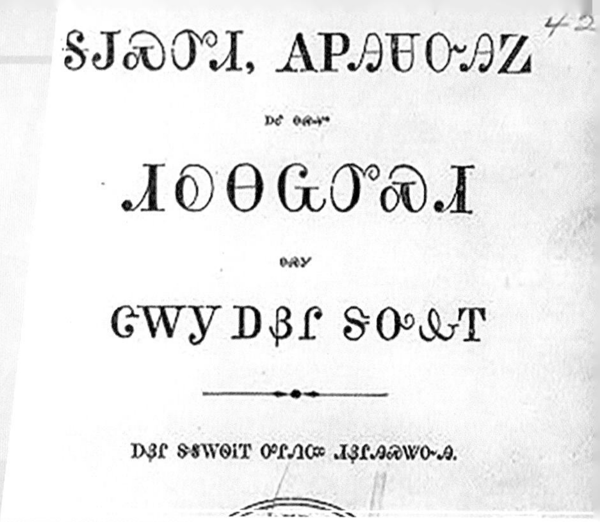

Parents & Visitors
SOUTH ENTRANCE
Cherokee Central Schools
September
13, 2009
RAVENSFORD DR.

Glossary

blacksmith—a person who makes or repairs things made of iron

communicated—to have given information about something to someone else

constitution—a system of beliefs and laws by which a country is governed

culture—the beliefs and ways of a group of people

customs—traditional behaviors or actions of a group of people

military—relating to soldiers and the armed forces

preserve—to keep something safe and in good condition

settlers—people who go to live in a new place where there are few other people

translated—changed from one language to another language

Index

Your Turn!

Forced to Leave

The U.S. government forced the Cherokee people to give up their land. They were tired, hungry, and sick. Thousands died. Write a poem that tells what you would feel if you were forced to leave your home.